Easter Sto

A Christian Bible Storybook for Children Aged 8-12
- Ideal for Sunday Schools and Easter Bible Study

BY

PUBLISHING

Copyright © [2025 by Graham Talbot

All rights reserved.

No part of this book may be reproduced, stored in a retrieval system, or transmitted in any form or by any means, electronic, mechanical, photocopying, recording, or otherwise, without the prior written permission of the publisher, except for brief quotations used in reviews or articles.

Dedication

This book is dedicated to every child who is learning to follow jesus and to everyone who is discovering the amazing love of god through him.

Welcome To The Easter Story!

Easter is the most important celebration for Christians. It's a story about incredible love, sacrifice, and victory. It's the story of Jesus, who came to show us God's love by teaching, healing, and performing miracles. But the most amazing part is what He did for us at the end of His life.

Jesus chose to die on a cross to forgive our sins. He didn't deserve to die, but He did it because He loves us. But the story doesn't end there! Three days after His death, Jesus came back to life — showing us that death could not defeat Him. His resurrection is a gift of new life for all who believe in Him.

In this book, you'll walk with Jesus through His final days, from His arrival in Jerusalem to His amazing resurrection. You'll learn about His love, His teachings, and the way He gave everything for us. The Easter story is not just for the past — it's for us today. It shows us how we can follow Jesus and live with hope, courage, and love.

How Can You Be Part of the Easter Story?

As you read through the chapters in this book, remember: the Easter story is not just something you read about — it's something you can live out. It's a story of love, sacrifice, and hope. And the best part is, you can be part of it! Jesus showed us how to love others, even when it's hard. He showed us how to forgive, to help, and to bring joy into the lives of those around us.

You can be part of the Easter story every day, whether you're at church, at home, at school, or with your friends. Every time you choose kindness, share love, or forgive, you are living the story of Easter. Just like Jesus did, you can help make the world a better place by following Him.

So as you walk through the pages of this book, think about how His story can change your life today — and how you can share His love with others, now and always. Are you ready to begin? Let's dive into the Easter story and see how it can transform you!

List of Contents

The Triumphal Entry	01
Jesus Cleanses the Temple	05
The Plot to Kill Jesus	09
The Last Supper	13
Jesus Washes His Disciples' Feet	17
Jesus Predicts Peter's Denial	21
Jesus Prays in the Garden	26
Jesus is Betrayed and Arrested	30
Jesus is Tried by the Religious Leaders	34
Peter Denies Jesus	38
Jesus is Sent to Pilate	42
Jesus is Crucified	47
Jesus' Death and Burial	51
The Resurrection	54
Jesus Appears to His Disciples	58
Jesus Appears to Thomas	61
Jesus Appears on the Shore	66
Jesus Restores Peter	72
Jesus Gives the Great Commission	77
The Ascension of Jesus	82

Chapter 1
The Triumphal Entry

It was a busy time in Jerusalem. People from all over had traveled to the city for the Passover festival, a time when everyone remembered how God had rescued His people from Egypt long ago. The city streets were crowded with excitement, and everyone was waiting for something special to happen. Little did they know, someone very special was about to arrive.

The air was filled with whispers, "Is He coming? Is He really coming today?" And there, in the distance, riding on a donkey, was Jesus.

Now, this wasn't just any man. Jesus had done incredible

things. He had healed the sick, made blind people see, and even raised people from the dead! People were starting to wonder if this might be the One they had been waiting for, the Messiah—the promised King who would come and save them.

As He drew nearer, the excitement grew. People began to rush out to meet Him. But instead of waiting for Jesus to come in a grand, royal way, like most kings, Jesus was riding on a humble donkey. Not a horse, not a chariot—just a simple donkey. Why? Because Jesus was showing that He wasn't a king who came to fight battles with soldiers. He was a King who came to bring peace.

People began shouting with joy and waving palm branches—branches from the palm trees that lined the streets. Some even took off their coats and laid them down on the ground like a red carpet for Him. It was as though they were welcoming a king, but they didn't understand that the kind of king Jesus was, was very different.

As Jesus rode through the streets, the people cried out:
"Hosanna! Hosanna to the Son of David! Blessed is He who comes in the name of the Lord!"
"Hosanna!" means "save us!" and the people were shouting because they believed Jesus was the one who could save them, the King who would set everything right. They were filled with hope. Could it be? Could this man riding on a donkey be the one to lead them into a new future?

But what was so special about the donkey? Why not a grand horse or chariot? The donkey was a symbol of peace. It wasn't a powerful warhorse used by mighty generals—it was a quiet, gentle animal. Jesus was showing everyone that He was a King of Peace, not a king who would conquer through fighting, but through love, forgiveness, and humility.

The people didn't fully understand this yet, but that's exactly why Jesus had come. He wasn't here to rule with an army or take control with power. He came to show people what it truly meant to live in God's kingdom—a kingdom where peace, love, and mercy are the most powerful things.

As He entered Jerusalem, the crowd's cheers were loud, and the streets were filled with excitement. Yet, not everyone was happy. The religious leaders, who should have been welcoming Jesus, were worried. They didn't like the way the crowds were praising Him. They didn't understand that the Messiah was not coming to take over the way they thought He would.

Still, Jesus kept riding. He knew the path ahead would not be easy. He knew that the people's joy today might quickly turn into sorrow in the days to come. But He also knew that this was part of God's plan—a plan that would change the world forever.

And so, the crowds continued to shout, waving their palm branches, as Jesus passed by. They didn't know what was going to happen next. But what they did know was that they were seeing something amazing, something that had been promised long ago.

The prophet Zechariah had said that the Messiah would come to Jerusalem, not in a way people expected, but riding humbly on a donkey. Jesus was fulfilling this ancient prophecy, showing everyone that God's plan was always in motion—even when people couldn't see it.

Jesus didn't come to be a king like the ones the people were used to. He wasn't going to fight wars or build an earthly empire. No, Jesus came to show a new way to live—a way of peace, love, and forgiveness. And that was the greatest thing He could offer to the world.

As the crowd cheered and waved their palm branches, they celebrated more than they realized. They were welcoming not just a king—but a Savior.

Chapter 2
Jesus Cleanses The Temple

The temple in Jerusalem was a beautiful place. It was meant to be a special place where people could come and be close to God, to pray, worship, and thank Him for all He had done. But something had gone terribly wrong.

When people traveled from far away to come to the temple, they would bring money to give to God as a gift. Some of them needed to buy animals for sacrifices, like doves or lambs, to offer to God. Normally, these animals were sold in a part of the temple area. But lately, something had changed.

Instead of a peaceful, quiet place of worship, the temple had become noisy and busy. Everywhere you looked, there were merchants selling animals, shouting prices, and arguing over money. The sound of coins clinking filled the air as money changers exchanged money for people who didn't have the right kind of coins. The smells of animals and the hustle of buying and selling made the temple feel more like a busy market than a holy place.

One day, Jesus came to the temple. He had been there many times before, but today, something was different. As He walked into the temple courts, He saw what had been happening. The noise, the animals, the people yelling—it was all too much. This wasn't the way God's house was meant to be. The temple wasn't supposed to be a place where people made money; it was meant to be a place to honor and worship God.

Jesus was angry, but not in the way we often think of anger. His anger was not about being hurt or upset personally. It was because He saw how the holiness of God's house had been disrespected. People were using it for their own selfish purposes instead of treating it as a place to meet with God.

And so, Jesus did something that shocked everyone. He began to drive out the merchants and the money changers. He turned over the tables where people had been sitting, exchanging money. Coins scattered everywhere! He picked up a whip and used it to chase the animals and people out of the temple courts.

He said loudly, "It is written, 'My house will be called a house of prayer,' but you are making it a 'den of robbers!'"

The people who had been there must have been stunned. They couldn't believe their eyes! Jesus, the kind and gentle teacher they had seen heal the sick and love the poor, was now showing anger—but it was righteous anger. It was the kind of anger that comes when something important has been disrespected.

The religious leaders and temple officials were furious. They didn't like what Jesus had done. How could He treat the temple this way? But Jesus wasn't just mad at the mess in the temple; He was upset because worshiping God should always come first. The temple was a place for people to be with God, not a place for business deals.

After driving out the merchants and money changers, Jesus reminded everyone why the temple existed in the first place. It wasn't for making money or selling things. It was for prayer, worship, and connecting with God.

As He did this, Jesus was teaching us something important. When we go to church or any place of worship, it's not about the things we can buy or sell or the things that distract us. What matters most is our hearts and our desire to be close to God. Jesus wanted everyone to remember that the house of God should always be a place of holiness and peace.

Later, when Jesus' disciples remembered what He had done,

they realized that He was fulfilling another part of the scriptures. The prophet Zeal had said, "Zeal for your house will consume me." Jesus was so passionate about honoring God's house that He took action when He saw it being misused. It wasn't just about the temple; it was about reverence—showing respect for God, and treating His holy things with care.

But the religious leaders didn't understand. They were so focused on their own rules and power that they couldn't see why Jesus did what He did. They didn't realize that He was trying to show them what truly mattered: a pure heart before God. He didn't want their worship to be a business; He wanted their worship to be real, to come from a place of love and respect for God.

The crowd was shocked, and so were the leaders. But despite their anger, Jesus' message was clear. When we come before God—whether in church, at home, or anywhere else—we are entering into a sacred space. It's a place for us to listen, to pray, to connect with the One who loves us more than we can imagine.

Chapter 3
The Plot to Kill Jesus

The days were getting darker in Jerusalem. Jesus had been teaching with great power, healing the sick, and speaking of God's Kingdom in ways no one had ever heard before. People were beginning to believe He was the Messiah—the Savior sent by God to rescue them. But not everyone was happy about this.

The religious leaders, the chief priests, and the teachers of the law, who were supposed to be the ones helping people understand God, were growing more and more angry with Jesus. He was challenging everything they had taught, and people were starting to follow Him instead of them. They felt their power slipping away. They were afraid that Jesus was going to take away their position in the community, and they couldn't let that happen.

They started to whisper among themselves. "What should we do with this man? He is making trouble! People are listening to Him. If we let Him continue, we might lose everything we have worked for."

Their jealousy turned into fear. They had power, and they didn't want to give it up. So, they began to plot. They were determined to get rid of Jesus. But they didn't want to do it in public, where the crowds would see. The people loved Jesus, and they feared the people's reaction. So they made a plan to arrest Him secretly. But how could they do that?

At that very time, one of Jesus' own disciples, someone who had been with Him through everything, came to them with an offer. His name was Judas.

Judas had been one of the twelve disciples, the close friends of Jesus. He had seen Jesus heal people, feed thousands, and teach about God's love. But for some reason, Judas began to feel discontent. He may have thought that Jesus wasn't the kind of king he had hoped for—a mighty warrior who would free the Jewish people from their enemies. Or maybe, like the religious leaders, he was afraid of losing his place, his position among the disciples, his reputation.

Judas went to the religious leaders and said, "What will you give me if I help you arrest Jesus? I will hand Him over to you."

The leaders looked at each other, surprised and pleased. They had been looking for a way to arrest Jesus, and now here was someone from inside His circle willing to help them. Judas didn't want much—just thirty pieces of silver.

The leaders agreed, and Judas made a secret deal with them. He would point out Jesus to them when the time was right, when Jesus was alone and away from the crowds. Then, they could arrest Him without anyone seeing.

Judas' decision to betray Jesus for silver was a tragic one. He had walked with Jesus, listened to His words, and witnessed His miracles. But in the end, he chose money over friendship, over love, over doing what was right. He didn't understand that following Jesus meant more than just being part of something big or important—it meant making hard choices and loving others the way Jesus loved him.

So, while the religious leaders were planning their secret plot to arrest Jesus, Judas was already making his deal. He was willing to turn his back on the One who had called him a friend.

As the days passed, Jesus knew that something was wrong. He had already been telling His disciples that hard times were coming, and He knew that He was walking toward something difficult, something painful. But He also knew that God's plan was bigger than anything they could understand.

One evening, as Jesus was teaching His disciples, He said, "One of you will betray Me." The disciples were shocked. They looked at each other in confusion and disbelief. "Who could it be?" they asked. "Not me, Lord, surely not me!"

But Jesus knew. He knew what Judas had already decided. He knew Judas would choose betrayal. Yet, even then, Jesus didn't speak harshly to him. He loved Judas all the same. He offered forgiveness, even though He knew what was about to happen.

Why did the religious leaders fear Jesus so much? Why did Judas betray Him? They feared that Jesus was too different from what they expected a king to be. Jesus was about love and truth, not power and control. He was changing everything, and the people who were in charge didn't want things to change. Judas, on the other hand, felt the weight of his own desires and fears, and he made a choice that would cost him dearly.

This chapter teaches us a difficult lesson. Sometimes, people choose to go against what is right because of fear, because of selfishness, or because they think they will gain something in the end. Judas betrayed Jesus for thirty pieces of silver, but in the end, he realized that what he had traded wasn't worth it. Nothing is worth more than the love and friendship of Jesus.

Chapter 4
The Last Supper

It was the night before something very important was going to happen. Jesus knew that His time on earth was coming to an end, and He wanted to share a very special meal with His friends, His disciples. This was no ordinary meal. It was the Passover, a time when the Jewish people remembered how God had saved them from slavery in Egypt many, many years ago. It was a time to thank God for His great love and protection.

Jesus and His disciples gathered together in a small room in the city of Jerusalem. The table was set with bread, wine, and all the traditional food that people ate during the Passover meal. Everyone was excited. This meal was an important part of their tradition, and the disciples knew that they would be remembering something special.

As they sat down, Jesus looked around at His friends. He knew what was about to happen—He knew He would soon have to face terrible things—but He also knew this meal would be the last time He could share this moment with them in this way. It was His chance to teach them something important, something that would help them understand all that He had done for them and all that was about to happen.

Then, as they ate together, Jesus did something unexpected. He picked up a loaf of bread and broke it into pieces. The disciples looked at Him, wondering what He was doing. Jesus looked at them with love in His eyes and said, "This is My body, which is given for you. Do this in remembrance of Me."

The disciples were confused. What did He mean? They had always celebrated Passover with bread, but now Jesus was saying that this bread represented His body? His body that would soon be broken?

Jesus wasn't just talking about the bread itself; He was talking about what it represented. Jesus was about to give His life for the world. His body would be broken, and He wanted them to understand that this bread, shared among friends, was a symbol of the sacrifice He would soon make on the cross. It was a way for them to remember the love He had for them—a love so great that He would give everything, even His life.

After sharing the bread, Jesus took a cup filled with wine. He held it up and said, "This cup is the new covenant in My blood, which is poured out for you."

The disciples must have stared at the cup, even more confused than before. What was this new covenant Jesus was talking about? They had heard about covenants before—God had made promises with His people throughout history, but now Jesus was saying that this was something new. A new promise. A new way to be close to God.

Jesus explained that the wine in the cup represented His blood, which would be poured out for them. The blood of animals had been used in sacrifices for hundreds of years to cover people's sins, but Jesus was about to do something different. His sacrifice would not just cover sins for a moment; His sacrifice would forgive them forever.

This new covenant was the promise that Jesus' death would take away the need for any more sacrifices. His blood would be the final sacrifice, the one that would wash away the sins of the world. And Jesus wanted His disciples—and all who would follow Him after them—to remember this, every time they ate the bread and drank the wine.

As Jesus shared this meal with His friends, He was not just giving them food; He was giving them a way to remember Him and the sacrifice He was about to make. He was teaching them how to remember His love, His forgiveness, and the new life that He would offer through His death and resurrection.

"You will not see Me again until the Kingdom of God comes," He said. This wasn't just a goodbye; it was a promise. A promise that even though He was going away, He would be with them in a new way, through the Holy Spirit. And whenever they ate the bread and drank the wine, they would be reminded of that love and sacrifice. They would remember His body and blood, broken and poured out for them.

But Jesus wasn't only thinking about the disciples who were sitting at the table with Him that night. He was thinking about everyone—everyone—who would come to believe in Him. Through this meal, He was giving them a way to be connected to Him forever. He was offering communion—a way to come together as His followers and share in His love.

Chapter 5
Jesus Washes His Disciples' Feet

It was a quiet evening, and the air was thick with the warm smells of the meal they had just shared. The disciples sat around the table, chatting softly among themselves. They had been with Jesus for some time now, learning from Him, watching Him perform miracles, and hearing Him speak about God's Kingdom. They loved Him dearly, and they respected Him as their teacher and Lord.

But something was different about this evening. Jesus was about to do something that would surprise everyone. As the meal came to an end, the disciples looked around, realizing there was no one to wash their feet. Back then, it was a common custom to wash your feet before entering a house or eating, especially after walking through dusty streets. However, the disciples were too proud to offer to do it for each other.

They glanced at one another, not knowing who would take on the task. It was a job meant for servants, and no one wanted to be the servant in the room.

That's when Jesus stood up. Quietly, He left the table and walked over to a bowl of water. Without saying a word, He removed His outer robe and wrapped a towel around His waist, like a servant would. The disciples watched in silence, wondering what He was doing.

Jesus began to fill a basin with water and, one by one, knelt down in front of each disciple, gently lifting their feet and washing away the dust. The room was filled with awe and surprise. Here was Jesus—The Teacher, their Master—acting as the servant. This was a job no one expected Him to do. After all, wasn't He their leader? Wasn't He the one they looked up to?

When He came to Peter, Peter was taken aback. He couldn't believe what he was seeing. "Lord, You're going to wash my feet?" he asked, his voice trembling. Peter thought this act was too humble for Jesus, too lowly for someone so special. He couldn't accept it.
But Jesus answered him, "You don't understand what I'm doing right now, but you will later."

Peter, still shocked, protested, "No, Lord! You will never wash my feet!"

Jesus looked at him with gentle eyes and said, "Unless I wash you, you have no part with Me."

Suddenly, Peter understood. This wasn't just about his feet being clean. Jesus was doing something much more important. "Then, Lord," Peter exclaimed, "wash not just my feet, but my hands and my head too!"

Jesus smiled and shook His head gently. "Those who have already bathed are clean. You don't need a full bath, just your feet washed."

The other disciples were still processing everything that had happened. They had been following Jesus for so long, but this act of humility was beyond anything they had ever expected. The one who had taught them about the Kingdom of God, the one who had healed the sick and raised the dead, was now washing their feet. Jesus was showing them a lesson that would last forever.

When Jesus finished, He stood up and took off the towel. He returned to His seat at the table, and then He asked, "Do you understand what I have done for you?"
The disciples remained quiet. They didn't fully understand yet, but they knew something significant had taken place. Jesus continued, "You call Me 'Teacher' and 'Lord,' and you are right,

because that is what I am. But now that I, your Teacher and Lord, have washed your feet, you should also wash one another's feet."

The disciples sat in stunned silence. They had just seen Jesus do the most unexpected thing. The King of the world, their Savior, had acted as a servant. He had humbled Himself, and in doing so, He had shown them the true meaning of greatness. It wasn't about power or importance—it was about loving others and serving them.

Jesus wasn't asking them to literally wash each other's feet every day, though that would be a good act of kindness. He was telling them that true greatness in God's Kingdom is found in serving others with love, no matter their position or status. He wanted them to remember that, just as He had humbled Himself, they too should humble themselves for the sake of others.

"I have set an example for you," Jesus said. "Now you should do as I have done. If you know these things, you will be blessed if you do them."

As the disciples sat quietly, their hearts were filled with the power of what Jesus had shown them. They began to understand that true leadership in God's eyes is not about being in charge—it's about being the first to serve, the first to give, and the first to love.

Chapter 6
Jesus Predicts Peter's Denial

It was a quiet night, but a heavy feeling hung in the air. The disciples could sense that something was about to happen—something big. Jesus had been talking to them about strange things, things they didn't fully understand. He spoke of going away, of trouble coming, and of things that made their hearts uneasy. But among all of this, one of the disciples, Peter, had made something very clear: he would never leave Jesus. He loved Jesus too much to turn away.

"I will never leave You!" Peter had said with great passion. "Even if everyone else does, I will stay with You, no matter what!"

Jesus looked at Peter, His eyes filled with sadness and love. He knew what was coming, and He gently told Peter something that would change his life forever.

"Peter," Jesus said softly, "before the rooster crows tomorrow morning, you will deny Me three times."

Peter was shocked. He couldn't believe what he was hearing. "No, Lord!" he exclaimed. "I would never deny You. I love You too much! I would never say I don't know You."

The other disciples were listening, and they were all confused. How could this be? Peter, the one who had always been so strong and sure, was now being told he would deny Jesus?

But Jesus, who knew everything, looked at Peter with loving eyes and said, "Peter, I tell you the truth, before the rooster crows, you will deny Me three times. But don't be afraid. I will never stop loving you."

Peter, determined not to let Jesus down, said, "Even if I have to die with You, I will never deny You!"

The other disciples also said the same thing, all of them promising they would stand by Jesus no matter what.

But deep in their hearts, they didn't fully understand what was about to unfold. They didn't know that in just a few hours, everything would change. They didn't know that the trial and suffering Jesus was about to face would test their hearts in ways they never expected.

Later that night, after they had left the meal and were walking together to the garden, the disciples were still talking about Jesus' words. They didn't understand the weight of what was coming. They didn't know that Peter, the one who had always been so sure of himself, would face a test like no other.

When they arrived at the garden, Jesus asked the disciples to pray with Him. But Peter, along with the others, couldn't stay awake. The weight of the night was too much, and soon, they all fell asleep.

Jesus, on the other hand, prayed alone, feeling the pain of what was ahead. He knew that the time had come. He knew that the path to the cross was getting closer and closer. It wasn't going to be easy. It wasn't going to be painless. But Jesus knew this was the way to save the world.

Suddenly, in the darkness of the garden, a crowd of soldiers came toward them, led by Judas, one of the disciples who had betrayed Jesus. Judas kissed Jesus on the cheek, a sign to the soldiers that He was the one they were to arrest.

Peter, still confused and upset, drew his sword and tried to fight the soldiers. But Jesus stopped him. "Put your sword away," He said. "This is God's plan."

The soldiers took Jesus away, and the disciples scattered in fear. It was then that Peter's fear began to rise. He had promised he would never leave Jesus, but now, everything was falling apart. He didn't know what to do.

Peter followed the soldiers from a distance, not sure where they were taking Jesus. He came to a courtyard where people were gathered around a fire, talking and watching what was happening. Someone looked at Peter and said, "Aren't you one of Jesus' followers?"

Peter's heart raced. His mind was spinning. He couldn't let anyone know he was with Jesus. He couldn't bear to be arrested with Jesus. He had promised that he would stand by Jesus, but now fear was making him feel so small, so unsure of himself.

"I don't know what you're talking about," Peter said quickly, his voice shaking.

A little while later, another person came up to Peter and said, "You must be one of His followers. I can tell by the way you talk."

Peter's heart pounded in his chest. "No, I am not!" he insisted, his voice louder this time. He didn't want to be caught. He didn't want to suffer with Jesus.

But then, just as Jesus had said, it happened again. Someone else looked at Peter and said, "I'm sure you're one of Jesus' disciples."

Peter's fear exploded. "I don't know the man!" he shouted. He was terrified. How had it come to this? Just hours ago, he had promised that he would never leave Jesus, that he would never deny Him. And now, here he was, denying it all.

At that moment, the rooster crowed, just as Jesus had said it would. And Peter remembered. He remembered Jesus' words: "Before the rooster crows, you will deny Me three times." His heart sank, and he realized what he had done. He had failed Jesus. He had broken his promise.

Peter ran away, weeping bitterly. He was so sad and ashamed. He had failed the one person who had loved him so deeply. His heart was full of sorrow, and he couldn't stop crying. How could he ever forgive himself?

But even in Peter's brokenness, there was grace. Even though Peter had failed Jesus, Jesus never stopped loving him. He knew Peter's heart. He knew Peter's love. And in the days to come, Peter would find forgiveness and healing through the love of Jesus.

Chapter 7

Jesus Prays in the Garden

It was a quiet night in the garden of Gethsemane, and the stars twinkled brightly overhead. The moon cast a soft light on the peaceful trees, but in Jesus' heart, there was a storm. He walked slowly, His steps heavy with the weight of what was to come.

Jesus had asked His disciples to follow Him into the garden. They had seen Him teach crowds, heal the sick, and do so many wonderful things. But tonight was different. Tonight, they could sense that something was wrong. Still, they didn't fully understand what was going on.

"Stay here and keep watch with Me," Jesus told Peter, James, and John. He asked them to pray with Him, to stay awake with Him as He spoke with His Father in Heaven. He didn't want to face what was coming alone. These three disciples were His closest friends. He trusted them, but even they could not know the burden He carried.

He moved a little further into the garden, His heart heavy with sadness. Jesus knelt down on the soft ground, looking up to the night sky. He could feel the weight of everything He had taught, everything He had promised, and everything He was about to experience. His mind and heart were full of sorrow, and He knew the time had come for Him to make the hardest choice of all.

"Father, if there is any way, let this cup pass from Me," Jesus prayed quietly, His voice trembling. "But not My will, but Yours be done."

The "cup" He spoke of wasn't a literal cup, but a symbol of the suffering that awaited Him. Jesus knew the pain, the rejection, and the darkness that lay ahead. He knew He was about to face something no one else could bear. Yet, His heart trusted God.

He paused for a moment, looking up at the sky. The garden was so still, but inside, Jesus was wrestling with fear. His heart wanted to avoid the pain, but His love for the people He came to save was even greater. Jesus knew that God's plan would lead to a cross—but He also knew it was the only way to bring healing and forgiveness to the world.

After a while, Jesus stood up and walked back toward His disciples. He was hoping they had been praying with Him, staying awake to support Him. But when He reached them, He found them asleep.

"Couldn't you stay awake with Me for just one hour?" He asked softly. "Watch and pray so that you don't fall into temptation. The spirit is willing, but the body is weak."

The disciples stirred awake, rubbing their eyes, but their minds were heavy with sleep. They had no idea what was happening in the garden, no idea how close Jesus was to His moment of decision. Jesus didn't scold them, though. He simply returned to pray again.

He knelt down and prayed once more, the words still full of sorrow: "Father, if there is no other way, then I will do it. I will drink from the cup You have given Me."

As Jesus prayed, the weight of the world seemed to press on His shoulders. But still, He chose obedience. He knew God's plan was perfect, even though it meant pain. He trusted that God's way, though difficult, was the right path.

He returned to His disciples again, only to find them asleep once more. They had been so tired, so exhausted from the events of the day, that they had fallen asleep without realizing how much their Master needed them.

"Are you still sleeping and resting?" Jesus asked, though His voice was gentle. "The time has come. The one who will betray Me is near."

Even as He spoke these words, Jesus knew that the plan was set into motion. He would soon face His betrayer, and everything that was meant to happen would take place. But Jesus didn't fight it. He didn't run away. He simply stood, trusting that God's will was what was best for all.

"Get up. Let's go. The one who is going to betray Me is coming," Jesus said with calm strength.

Though He faced a future full of pain and fear, Jesus didn't shrink back. He trusted God completely and followed the path laid before Him, knowing it was the only way to bring salvation to everyone.

Chapter 8
Jesus is Betrayed and Arrested

The night in the garden of Gethsemane was still, but the air felt heavy. Jesus had just told His disciples that the time had come. He had shared His heart with them, even though they didn't fully understand. Jesus knew that what would happen next was part of God's big plan. But even so, it was going to be very hard.

As they walked back from the garden, the darkness felt deeper than it had before. The disciples were still trying to keep up, but their minds were racing. Something was wrong, but they couldn't put their finger on it. The quiet night felt too quiet—something was about to happen.

Suddenly, there was a noise in the distance—footsteps. The sound grew louder, and soon, they could see torches flickering in the dark. A crowd of people, holding sticks and swords, appeared. They were coming straight toward Jesus.

"Who is it you want?" Jesus asked, standing tall.

The soldiers didn't answer right away. They looked at Jesus, but then one man stepped forward. It was Judas. The man who had followed Jesus for so long. The man who had seen Jesus perform miracles, heal the sick, and speak words of love. Yet, Judas had chosen a different path.

Judas walked toward Jesus, and with a sad look in his eyes, he gave Jesus a kiss—a sign that Jesus was the one the soldiers were looking for.

"Judas, are you betraying the Son of Man with a kiss?" Jesus asked softly, His voice full of sadness, but not anger. Jesus had known for a long time that Judas would make this choice, but it still hurt Him. The one who had been a friend, the one who had shared meals with Jesus, was now the one who would help the soldiers take Jesus away.

The disciples were shocked. They couldn't believe what was happening. They had spent so much time with Jesus, following Him, learning from Him, and now one of them was going to turn against Him. It didn't make sense. Why would Judas do this? Why would anyone betray someone as kind and loving as Jesus?

Before anyone could speak, the soldiers stepped forward to arrest Jesus. The disciples were confused and scared. Peter, always quick to act, drew his sword and swung it at one of the soldiers. But Jesus stopped him.

"Put your sword back in its place," Jesus said, His voice calm yet firm. "For all who draw the sword will die by the sword."

The disciples didn't understand what Jesus meant. They were frightened. How could Jesus just stand there, ready to be arrested? Why wasn't He fighting back? But Jesus wasn't afraid. He knew that this was the moment when God's plan would begin to unfold.

Jesus turned to the soldiers and said, "Am I leading a rebellion, that you have come with swords and clubs? Every day I was with you, teaching in the temple, and you didn't arrest Me. But this is your hour, when darkness reigns."

The soldiers didn't answer. They just grabbed hold of Jesus and began to take Him away. The disciples watched, helpless and confused, as their Teacher, their Friend, was arrested like a criminal.

One by one, they all began to run. They were scared, and they didn't want to be caught. They had no idea what to do. The man they had followed so closely, the man who had healed the sick and made the blind see, was now being taken away. It was hard to believe.

Jesus, however, walked calmly through it all. His eyes were filled with peace, knowing that He was not only surrendering to the soldiers, but also to God's will. He wasn't afraid, even though everything around Him seemed to be falling apart.

As Jesus was led away, He said to His disciples, "This is the way it must be. This is the plan God has for me, and it will be done."

The disciples, still shocked, watched as Jesus disappeared into the night, His figure fading in the distance. They had no idea what the next hours would bring, but one thing was certain: Jesus was showing them something they would never forget. He was showing them courage like no one had ever seen before.

Chapter 9
Jesus Is Tried By The Religious Leaders

It was late at night, and the air in the chamber was thick with murmurs and hurried footsteps. The city of Jerusalem was still, but behind the walls of the high priest's house, there was an uneasy hum. The religious leaders, the ones who had once been respected by all, were now consumed with one singular thought: how could they rid themselves of this man, Jesus?

They had watched Him for days, hearing His teachings, watching His miracles, and seeing how the crowds followed Him. They felt their power slipping away. Jesus wasn't like the teachers of the law or the Pharisees—they could not control Him, and His words seemed to stir something deeper in the people.

He spoke with authority, as if He knew God intimately—because He did.

Now, it was time to make a decision. The leaders had been plotting for some time, but tonight, they were finally acting. Their plan was clear: they needed to accuse Jesus of something so terrible that the crowds would no longer follow Him, and the Romans would do their dirty work.

But no matter how hard they searched, no one could bring forward a truthful accusation. The witnesses they called could not agree on what Jesus had said or done. One said Jesus had threatened to destroy the temple, but when others tried to repeat the story, their words faltered. Lies fell apart when faced with the truth, but the leaders weren't willing to admit that. They were desperate.

The high priest, Caiaphas, grew impatient. He couldn't wait any longer. He approached Jesus, His hands raised in frustration. "Are you the Christ?" he demanded. "Are you the one who will come to save us?"

The room went still. The flickering light from the torches cast shadows on the walls, and everyone held their breath. Jesus, calm and unshaken, looked at him directly. "I am," He answered. "And you will see the Son of Man sitting at the right hand of the Mighty One and coming on the clouds of heaven."

Caiaphas' face twisted in disbelief. In a fit of anger, he ripped his robes, a sign of utter outrage. "Blasphemy!" he cried. "Do we need any more witnesses? You've heard it with your own ears—this man claims to be God!"

The crowd erupted in a frenzy, shouting loudly, accusing Jesus of terrible things. They wanted blood. They wanted Him to be punished. The room was filled with shouting and chaos as the leaders turned on Him, their hearts full of hatred. They had found their reason—their excuse to silence Him.

Meanwhile, Jesus stood there, unmoving, His face calm and serene. He didn't fight back. He didn't raise His voice. He simply stood, knowing that God's will was unfolding. He had known this moment would come, and He knew that His silence spoke louder than any words He could have spoken.

The guards, eager to please their masters, came forward to punish Jesus. They mocked Him. They blindfolded Him, hitting Him with their fists. "Prophesy, who struck you?" they sneered. But Jesus didn't respond. He didn't shout in anger or cry out in pain. He endured it all, knowing that He was walking the path God had set before Him.

Outside, the disciples had scattered. They couldn't bear to watch. They were terrified, unable to understand how this could be happening. They had seen Jesus heal the sick and raise the dead, and yet, here He was, standing silently before His accusers. But in this moment, they couldn't see the full picture. They didn't understand that this was part of God's great plan—the plan to save the world.

Jesus, knowing what was to come, didn't resist. He had chosen this path, not because it was easy, but because it was necessary. He had come to give His life for those who needed salvation. And even though His own people rejected Him, Jesus still loved them, still prayed for them, and still trusted God's plan.

Chapter 10
Peter Denies Jesus

It was a cold and lonely night. The sky was dark, and a chill hung in the air as Peter stood near a fire, warming his hands. The crackling of the flames couldn't quiet the storm raging inside him.

He had promised Jesus that he would never deny Him. "Even if everyone else turns away from You, I will stay with You," Peter had said just hours before, full of confidence and love. But now, standing in the courtyard of the high priest's house, everything felt different.

Peter had followed Jesus after He was arrested, unsure of what to do, yet unwilling to leave Him completely. He kept his distance from the guards and tried to blend in with the crowd, hoping that no one would notice him. But as the night went on, his heart began to race. He had been close to Jesus for so long—he had seen Jesus heal the sick, calm the storm, and even raise the dead. How could he be here now, in this cold place, while his friend and Savior was being put on trial?

A young servant girl suddenly appeared in front of Peter. Her eyes studied him for a moment before she spoke. "You were with that Jesus from Nazareth, weren't you?"

Peter's heart skipped a beat. He felt the weight of her words, like a heavy stone pressing down on his chest. He looked at her, and without thinking, he shook his head. "I don't know what you're talking about," he said quickly, his voice a little too loud, a little too nervous. "I'm not one of His followers."

He turned away, hoping she would let it go, but something inside him felt wrong. He knew he had just lied. Peter tried to push the feeling aside, but it clung to him, like a shadow he couldn't escape.

The night seemed to drag on. The fire crackled, and the voices of the crowd around him grew louder. Peter's eyes darted nervously from one face to the next. Could anyone tell what he had just done? He could feel his heart pounding in his chest.

Then, a little while later, another person came up to him. This time, it was a man, someone who had seen Peter in the garden, walking with Jesus. "Surely, you're one of them," the man said. "You're a Galilean, just like Him!"

Peter's stomach twisted. His mind raced, and for a moment, it felt like the whole world was closing in on him. He opened his mouth to speak, but no words came out. Then, desperate to silence the accusation, he blurted out, "I don't know the man!" His voice was sharp, and his words felt like a knife in his own heart. But Peter couldn't stop now. The fear was too much.

The others around him seemed satisfied, and for a moment, he thought he could breathe again. But deep down, he felt empty. The words echoed in his mind: "I don't know the man." How could he have said that? How could he have denied Jesus?

Then it happened. A third person approached Peter, and this time, the accusation was louder, more pointed. "You're one of His followers, aren't you? I can tell by the way you speak!"

Peter was terrified. His mind was a blur, and in a panic, he swore. "I don't know the man! I don't know Him!" His voice was shaking, and his face turned pale. He could hardly believe the words coming out of his mouth. How had he come to this? How had he gone from declaring his love for Jesus to denying Him in front of everyone?

At that very moment, a rooster crowed. Peter froze.

The sound of the rooster pierced through the night, and in that instant, something inside Peter broke. The words Jesus had spoken earlier came rushing back to him: "Before the rooster crows, you will deny Me three times."

Peter's heart sank. The guilt washed over him like a flood. He had failed. He had done the very thing he had promised never to do. He had denied the One who had loved him, who had called him to follow Him. Peter's hands trembled, and his eyes filled with tears. He looked around, hoping no one had seen his shame, but the truth was inside him. He could not escape it.

Peter turned away from the fire and hurried out into the darkness. He found a quiet corner, and there, hidden from the crowd, he sank to his knees. His tears fell freely now. How could he have done this? How could he have let fear control him and deny Jesus?

As the night wore on, Peter's thoughts were filled with regret. He felt as if he had failed completely, as though there was no way back. But in the quiet of his heart, a question lingered: Would Jesus forgive him? Could Jesus forgive him after everything?

Peter didn't have the answer, but he knew one thing for sure: he would never forget this night—the night when he had denied the One who had given him everything. And somehow, he knew that Jesus still loved him, even if he had failed. But could he ever be forgiven?

Chapter 11
Jesus Is Sent To Pilate

The sun was barely rising over Jerusalem when Jesus was brought before the governor, Pilate. The city was still, as though holding its breath, waiting to see what would happen next. Pilate's palace stood like a fortress at the edge of the city, its high walls casting long shadows. Inside, Jesus stood alone, His hands bound and His eyes steady.

Pilate looked at the man standing before him. He was puzzled. Jesus didn't look like the kind of man who deserved to be arrested. His face wasn't twisted in anger or fear, like most prisoners. Jesus was calm, even peaceful. There was no sign of rebellion in Him. And yet, here He was, standing before the governor of the land, accused of doing things He had not done.

The governor looked over at the chief priests and religious leaders who had brought Jesus to him. They were shouting, pointing at Jesus, accusing Him of stirring up trouble. They said He was claiming to be the King of the Jews, which Pilate knew would make the Roman authorities nervous. But Pilate wasn't sure. He looked at Jesus again.

"Are You the King of the Jews?" Pilate asked, his voice cold and curious. Jesus did not flinch. He simply looked back at Pilate with eyes full of quiet strength.

"You say so," Jesus replied.

Pilate was confused. This was not the answer he expected. He was used to prisoners pleading, arguing, or trying to defend themselves. But Jesus was different. There was no anger in Him, no fear. It was as though He knew exactly what was happening, even if no one else did.

Pilate turned to the crowd and the religious leaders. "I find no reason to execute this man," he said. "He has done nothing wrong."

But the crowd grew louder. They began to shout, chanting in unison. "Crucify Him! Crucify Him!" Their voices were filled with anger, and the noise seemed to fill the whole courtyard. The religious leaders stirred the crowd even more, making them demand Jesus' death.

Pilate felt a wave of pressure. He had hoped this would end quickly, but the crowd was relentless. He turned back to Jesus. "What is it You've done to make them so angry?" he asked. But Jesus remained silent. He didn't explain Himself, didn't argue. He simply stood there, as though He knew His time had come.

Pilate was troubled. He didn't want to execute an innocent man, but the crowd was becoming more dangerous by the minute. He thought for a moment and then came up with an idea. It was the custom for the Roman governor to release one prisoner at Passover, a gesture of goodwill toward the people. Perhaps he could use this to get out of the situation.

Pilate called for the prisoners to be brought forward. "It's your tradition that I release a prisoner to you at Passover," he said to the crowd. "Which one do you want me to release? Barabbas, the murderer and rebel? Or Jesus, who is called the Messiah?"

Pilate thought for sure they would choose Jesus. He was the innocent one, the one who had done no wrong. But the crowd roared with anger. "Give us Barabbas!" they shouted.

Pilate was shocked. "What should I do with Jesus, then?" he asked. But the crowd didn't care. "Crucify Him! Crucify Him!" they yelled even louder. The sound was deafening.

Pilate felt trapped. He had no way of stopping this. The pressure was mounting. He didn't want to anger the crowd or the religious leaders, but he also didn't want to condemn an innocent man. He knew Jesus wasn't guilty, but the people wanted Him dead.

In a final act of surrender, Pilate did something strange. He called for a basin of water and, in front of everyone, he washed his hands. "I am innocent of this man's blood," he said. "It is your responsibility." He handed the decision over to the crowd, hoping this would free him of the guilt he felt.

But the people didn't care. They were too caught up in their anger. "Let His blood be on us and on our children!" they cried. Pilate could do nothing. He had tried to make a fair decision, but the crowd had forced his hand.

Pilate turned to the soldiers and motioned for them to take Jesus away. "Do what you must," he said quietly.

And so, with a heavy heart and a mind full of doubt, Pilate allowed Jesus to be sent to His death. Jesus, the innocent One, would be crucified.

As the soldiers led Jesus away, Pilate couldn't help but wonder what kind of King Jesus was. He had seen many rulers and leaders in his life, but none of them had ever behaved like this. Jesus didn't fight back. He didn't beg for His life. He simply accepted His fate, as though He had known all along that this was part of the plan.

Pilate's decision would be remembered forever—not because it was a good decision, but because it showed how easily people could be swayed by fear and the crowd's pressure. Pilate had known what was right, but in the end, he let the voices of others drown out his conscience.

Jesus, on the other hand, had remained faithful to God's plan, even in the face of injustice. His path was one of obedience, not to the people, but to His Father.

Chapter 12
Jesus is Crucified

The hill outside the city was quiet, but the air felt heavy. It wasn't the usual stillness that comes with a peaceful morning. This was a silence that made everything feel wrong, like something terrible was about to happen. And it was.

Jesus, who had healed the sick and fed the hungry, who had given sight to the blind and shown kindness to everyone, was being led up that hill. He was carrying a heavy wooden cross on

His back, the weight of it making Him stumble under the burden. The soldiers, with their stern faces and sharp commands, didn't show any mercy. They were too focused on their orders.

The crowd had gathered at the foot of the hill. Some of them had followed Jesus when He had healed them. Others were there because they were curious or just wanted to see what would happen. But there were many who were shouting, "Crucify Him! Crucify Him!" These were the same voices that had called for His death just days before, demanding that the man who had done nothing wrong be punished in the worst way.

As Jesus was nailed to the cross, the sound of hammering rang out in the still air. The nails pierced His hands and feet, and the soldiers lifted the cross, dropping it into the hole that had been prepared for it. The crowd watched in silence now, some people weeping, others just staring. They couldn't believe what was happening. This man, who had done nothing but good, was being treated like a criminal.

Jesus hung there, His body in pain, the weight of His own body pulling down on His hands and feet. But in the midst of the pain, Jesus did something extraordinary. He looked at the people who had hurt Him, the ones who had nailed Him to that cross, and He spoke.

"Father, forgive them," He said, "for they do not know what they are doing."

Even as He suffered, Jesus prayed for the people who had put Him there. He prayed for forgiveness for those who had betrayed Him, for those who had shouted against Him, for those who had rejected Him. This was the heart of Jesus—loving, forgiving, even in the midst of His pain.

The sky grew darker. It wasn't just the evening shadows that made it dark, but a deep, unnatural darkness that seemed to cover the land. The sun hid its face, as though it could not bear to look at what was happening. For three long hours, the darkness covered everything, and Jesus hung on the cross, His body wracked with pain.

As the darkness deepened, Jesus spoke again, this time with words that made the earth tremble. "My God, My God, why have You forsaken Me?" His voice echoed through the empty air, filled with sorrow. It was a cry of deep loneliness, as though Jesus was feeling the weight of all the sin of the world pressing down on Him. For the first time, He felt separated from His Father. But even in that moment of anguish, Jesus didn't give up. He kept trusting in God's plan.

Then, in the final moments, as the darkness lifted, Jesus took a deep breath and said, "It is finished."

With those words, He knew the work He had come to do was done. His mission was complete. He had taken on the sins of the world, all the wrongs that everyone had ever done, and paid the price for them. The suffering was over, and the way for forgiveness was open to everyone who would believe.

As He spoke those words, the ground beneath Him shook. A great earthquake split the earth in two. The curtain in the temple, the curtain that separated the people from God, was torn from top to bottom. It was as though the very heavens themselves were reacting to what had just happened. Jesus had given His life as the final sacrifice, the one that would bring peace between God and people forever.

And then, with a final breath, Jesus bowed His head and gave up His spirit. He had finished His mission. He had done it out of love—love for everyone, even for those who had hurt Him.

As His body hung lifeless on the cross, the soldiers who had been guarding Him saw the earthquake and the dark sky. They were amazed. "Surely, this man was the Son of God!" one of them exclaimed. It was a moment of recognition, a moment when even the Roman soldiers, who had been part of the execution, understood that Jesus was not just a man, but the Son of God.

The crowd began to scatter, some of them shocked, some of them filled with grief. But for those who truly understood, the death of Jesus was not the end of the story. It was the beginning. Jesus had done what no one else could do. He had taken the punishment for sin upon Himself so that all who believe in Him could be forgiven and have eternal life with God.

Chapter 13
Jesus' Death and Burial

The day was drawing to a close, but something far greater than the setting sun was happening. Jesus, the Son of God, was hanging on the cross, His body bruised and broken. The crowd, which had once cheered for Him, now stood in stunned silence. Some of them wept quietly, some were still in shock, and others just couldn't understand how it had come to this.

As He hung there, Jesus spoke with His last strength, His voice soft but strong. "It is finished," He said. Those words were not words of defeat, but of victory. Jesus had come to earth to do something that no one else could do: He came to take the punishment for sin, so that everyone who believed in Him could be forgiven and set free. It was finished, because the task was complete. The price had been paid.

But what happened next was even more surprising. The sky, which had been so bright just hours earlier, suddenly turned dark—very dark, like the night had fallen early. It felt like the earth was mourning. The ground shook, and for a moment, everything seemed out of place.

One of the soldiers standing by the cross saw what happened, and he was amazed. He looked at Jesus and said, "Surely, this was the Son of God." He had seen many people die, but no one had died like this—no one had spoken words of forgiveness and love even as they were dying.

After Jesus gave His final words, He breathed His last breath, and the earth became still. His followers, who had been watching from a distance, could hardly believe what had happened. Their hearts were heavy. How could this be the end?

A man named Joseph of Arimathea, who had quietly followed Jesus, came to Pilate, the Roman governor. He asked if he could take Jesus' body down from the cross. Pilate agreed, and Joseph, along with a man named Nicodemus, took the body of Jesus and prepared it for burial.

They wrapped Jesus' body in a clean linen cloth and carried it to a tomb—a tomb that had been carved into a rock. It was a tomb where no one had ever been laid. They gently placed Jesus' body inside, and then, to make sure no one could steal the body, they rolled a large stone in front of the tomb.

The women who had been following Jesus—Mary Magdalene and Mary, the mother of James—watched from a distance. They knew that they would come back on the third day to anoint Jesus' body with spices, as was the custom. But for now, they stood still, hearts heavy with sorrow.

As the stone was rolled into place, a sense of finality hung in the air. Jesus was dead. His body lay in the tomb. And for His disciples, it felt like all their hopes and dreams had been shattered. They had followed Jesus for so long, and now it seemed like everything had come to an end.

But what they didn't know, what no one could have imagined, was that this was not the end. This was just the beginning.

Chapter 14

The Resurrection

The sun had barely begun to rise when Mary Magdalene, Mary the mother of James, and a few other women made their way toward the tomb. The path was quiet, the world still asleep, and the air was cool. The women were carrying sweet-smelling spices, planning to anoint Jesus' body, as they had seen others do before.

But as they neared the tomb, they noticed something strange. The stone that had been rolled in front of the tomb was no longer in place! It was rolled away—just like that. Their hearts raced with confusion. What could have happened? Had someone taken Jesus' body?

The women hurriedly looked inside the tomb, but it was empty. Jesus' body was gone! They were shocked and frightened, not knowing what to think.

Then, out of nowhere, a bright light suddenly appeared, and an angel of the Lord stood before them. The women froze, their hearts pounding in their chests. The angel's clothes shone as bright as lightning, and his face was like the sun itself. He spoke to them, his voice full of joy and peace:

"Do not be afraid! I know you are looking for Jesus, who was crucified. He is not here. He has risen, just as He said He would! Come, see where He lay."

The women's eyes widened. Was this really happening? Could it be true? The tomb, once dark and still, now seemed filled with light and hope. Jesus was alive!

The angel continued, "Now go quickly and tell His disciples. He is going ahead of you to Galilee. There you will see Him. Now I have told you."

With hearts full of joy and wonder, the women turned and ran. They couldn't wait to share the incredible news! As they hurried, they suddenly saw someone standing before them. It was Jesus! Alive! His face was full of love and warmth, just as they had remembered it.

"Greetings!" Jesus said, smiling at them.

The women fell to their knees, worshiping Him. They were trembling with awe, but also filled with indescribable joy. "Do not be afraid," Jesus told them, His voice so gentle and kind. "Go and tell my brothers to go to Galilee; there they will see Me."

The women rushed back to where the disciples were staying, their voices bubbling over with excitement. "Jesus is alive! We saw Him! The tomb is empty!" they cried. The disciples couldn't believe it at first. They thought it was too good to be true, and they didn't know what to think. But the women had seen Him, and they knew that something incredible had happened.

Suddenly, Jesus appeared again—this time, not just to the women, but to all the disciples. He stood in the middle of them, smiling. "Peace be with you," He said. The disciples couldn't believe their eyes. Here was Jesus, the One who had died on the cross, standing in front of them, alive!

Jesus showed them His hands and His side, the marks of His death still visible. He wasn't a ghost. He wasn't just a memory. He was alive, in the flesh, with them, just as He had promised.

The disciples were filled with joy, their fears and doubts melt ing away. Jesus was alive! Death had not defeated Him. He had conquered it. The victory was His, and He was alive forever!

Jesus then told them, "As the Father has sent Me, I am sending you." He gave them a mission: to go and share the good news of His resurrection with everyone, to tell the world that Jesus had defeated death and that through Him, everyone could have eternal life.

The disciples went out, filled with the power of the Holy Spirit, and began to spread the news far and wide. They had seen it for themselves: Jesus had risen from the dead! Nothing could ever be the same again.

Chapter 15

Jesus Appears to His Disciples

It was early in the evening, and the disciples were gathered together in a room, their hearts still full of wonder and confusion. The doors were locked, and they sat in silence, still trying to understand everything that had happened. They had heard the women tell them that Jesus was alive, but could it really be true? Could their friend—no, their Savior—really be back?

Suddenly, without warning, the room was filled with light. The disciples gasped in fear, but then they heard a familiar voice saying, "Peace be with you."

They looked up. There, standing before them, was Jesus!

At first, the disciples didn't know what to say. How could it be Him? Was this a dream? Were their eyes playing tricks on them? But then they saw His hands, His feet, and the scars from where the nails had pierced them. They could see the wound in His side, the mark of the spear that had gone through Him.

It was real. Jesus was standing in front of them, alive and full of peace.

"Why are you so frightened?" Jesus asked gently, smiling at them. "Look at My hands and My feet. It is really Me! Touch Me, and see. A ghost doesn't have flesh and bones like I do."

With shaking hands, they reached out, and one by one, they touched Jesus. His body was real, His wounds were real. He was not a ghost. He had truly risen from the dead, just as He had promised.

The disciples were filled with joy, but there was still a little doubt in their hearts. Jesus smiled and asked, "Do you have anything to eat?"

One of the disciples quickly brought Him some fish. Jesus took it and ate it in front of them. He was really alive! He wasn't just a spirit; He was fully alive, in a way they couldn't fully understand.

Then, Jesus spoke to them with a mission in His voice: "You are witnesses of these things. Everything that happened, everything I taught you, was for a reason. You are going to tell the world about Me. You will share the good news with everyone!"

Jesus' words made the disciples' hearts burn with excitement. They were going to be part of something huge—something that would change the world forever!

But Jesus wasn't finished. "I'm going to send you what My Father has promised," He said, referring to the Holy Spirit. "You will be filled with power, and then you will go to all nations, sharing My love and telling everyone about the resurrection."

The disciples felt both nervous and excited. It seemed like such a big job. Could they really do it? But Jesus reassured them, saying, "Don't be afraid. I am with you always. You will not be alone."

Before He left, Jesus blessed them with one final promise: "I will always be with you, even to the end of the age. Go, and make disciples of all nations. Teach them to obey everything I have commanded you."

And with those words, Jesus lifted up His hands and blessed them. Then, in the twinkling of an eye, He was gone. He didn't leave them in fear; He left them with hope, with a mission, and with a promise that He would always be with them.

Chapter 16
Jesus Appears to Thomas

It had been a whole week since the disciples had seen Jesus. They were all still amazed, their hearts overflowing with joy and wonder. Jesus had risen from the dead! He had appeared to them, showing them His hands and His side, the very places where the soldiers had nailed Him to the cross. They had heard His voice. They had touched His wounds. They had seen His living, breathing body. But one disciple, Thomas, wasn't with them when that first miraculous moment happened.

Thomas had been so sad and confused that evening. When the disciples found him and told him, "We have seen the Lord!" Thomas shook his head in disbelief. "I don't believe you," he said. "Unless I see the nail marks in His hands, unless I put my finger where the nails were, and put my hand into His side, I won't believe."

Thomas was known for his honesty, and though he felt disappointed and hurt, he couldn't just believe something without being sure. He was a man of truth, and to him, this sounded too impossible to believe. "I need to see it with my own eyes," Thomas thought. He wanted to know, really know, that Jesus was alive.

A week passed. It felt long for Thomas. He was still in the dark, still longing for the truth. He wasn't angry, but his heart felt heavy. He missed Jesus so much, and he couldn't understand what had happened.

That Sunday, Thomas was with the disciples again. They were gathered in a room, doors locked tight. They had done this before, waiting, hoping, unsure of what was next. But this time was different.

Suddenly, there He was.

Jesus appeared right in front of them! He stood there, alive, right before their eyes. The room was filled with light, as if the darkness itself had been banished. Jesus smiled at them, as if nothing had happened, as if He had simply stepped out of the shadows.

"Peace be with you!" He said, His voice as kind as ever.

The disciples' hearts jumped in excitement. But there was someone who hadn't yet seen. There was one disciple who was still in doubt. Thomas, standing in the corner, looked up slowly. He couldn't believe his eyes.

It was Jesus. He was standing right in front of him.

"Thomas," Jesus said, His eyes full of understanding. "Come here. Look at My hands. Put your finger where the nails were. Reach out and put your hand into My side. Stop doubting and believe."

Thomas stared in awe. There was no mistaking it. This was Jesus. The same Jesus who had been crucified, the same Jesus who had died on the cross. The wounds in His hands were still there, the scars from the nails. The wound in His side was still open. It was real. It wasn't a dream. It wasn't a trick. It was Jesus. Alive. Right there.

Thomas, though still in shock, took a small step forward. His eyes filled with tears. He had doubted, but now everything made sense. Jesus had risen. Jesus was alive. He didn't need to touch the wounds, didn't need to see the scars up close anymore. His heart told him everything.

"My Lord and my God!" Thomas exclaimed, his voice shaking with emotion.

Jesus smiled softly at Thomas and said, "Because you have seen Me, you have believed. But blessed are those who have not seen and yet have believed."

Thomas fell to his knees, overwhelmed by what had just happened. He had seen with his own eyes that Jesus was alive. But now, his heart was even more certain. Jesus had come to him, had shown him His wounds, had answered his doubts, and had called him to believe.

Jesus' words were not just for Thomas, but for all who would come after him. Even though we can't see Jesus with our eyes today, He promises that those who believe without seeing are blessed. And that includes us.

Thomas' faith was restored, but it didn't just stay in his heart. From that moment on, Thomas became one of the strongest witnesses of Jesus' resurrection. He went all over, telling everyone about what he had seen and believed. He shared his story with others, showing them that Jesus is alive. He didn't want anyone to live in doubt like he had. Thomas became a brave and bold preacher, telling everyone that Jesus is the Son of God, the Savior of the world.

The other disciples continued their work too. Together, they traveled, preaching and teaching about the good news of Jesus' resurrection. They knew that Jesus had risen from the dead and that He had conquered sin and death. They wanted to share that with everyone, so that others could believe, too.

But Thomas' story is special, because it reminds us of something very important. We all go through times when we doubt. We all face moments when we wonder, "Is God really there? Is He really alive? Does He really love me?" Just like Thomas, we sometimes need to see with our hearts, even when we can't see with our eyes.

In fact, Jesus calls us to have faith, even without seeing Him face to face. He asks us to trust Him, to believe in Him, and to follow Him, just like the disciples did after Thomas. He promises that those who believe in Him will be blessed, just as He promised Thomas.

So, whenever you feel unsure, whenever you wonder if God is with you, remember Thomas. He was once unsure, too. But when he saw Jesus, his heart changed forever. And Jesus will always help us grow in faith, just like He did for Thomas.

Chapter 17
Jesus Appears on the Shore

The early morning air was cool, and the sea was quiet. The disciples had been out all night, fishing, but they hadn't caught a thing. Their nets were empty, and their hearts were heavy. They were tired and frustrated. What were they supposed to do now? Jesus had risen from the dead, and they had seen Him, but what came next? The future was uncertain, and they felt lost.

Peter was the one who finally broke the silence. "I'm going fishing," he said. It wasn't a new idea. Before they had followed Jesus, many of them had been fishermen, and the sea was something they knew well. Maybe a day of fishing would clear their minds.

The others agreed. "We'll go with you," they said, and together they got into the boat and pushed off into the water. All night long, they cast their nets into the sea. Again and again, they pulled them up, hoping for a catch, but each time, the nets came back empty. There were no fish to be found.

By the time the sun began to rise, they were exhausted. The night had been long, and they felt like failures. Peter and the others sat in the boat, staring out at the water, wondering what they had done wrong.

Suddenly, they heard a voice from the shore. "Friends, haven't you any fish?"

The disciples looked up, squinting in the early morning light. There was a man standing on the shore, but they couldn't make out who it was. He didn't seem to be a fisherman, so how could he know they hadn't caught anything?

"No," they answered, feeling a little embarrassed. They had been out all night and hadn't caught a single fish.

The man on the shore then said something surprising. "Throw your net on the right side of the boat, and you will find some."

It was a strange suggestion. They had been fishing all night, and the idea of just trying one more time seemed a little silly.

But something about the man's voice made them listen. Maybe they thought it couldn't hurt. Maybe they remembered the first time Jesus had told them to cast their nets, and how that had led to a huge catch.

So, with a little shrug, they cast their nets onto the other side of the boat. And immediately, the nets became so full that they couldn't pull them back in. The fish were everywhere, jumping and wriggling in the net. It was a miracle!

That's when John, one of the disciples, looked at Peter and said, "It's the Lord!" His heart raced as he realized that the man on the shore was no stranger—it was Jesus!

When Peter heard these words, his heart skipped a beat. He was so excited, he didn't even wait for the boat to reach the shore. Without thinking, Peter jumped into the water, the cool waves splashing around him as he swam toward Jesus. His heart was full of joy and excitement. He couldn't wait to reach Jesus, to be with Him again.

The other disciples followed in the boat, towing the overflowing net behind them. When they reached the shore, they saw that Jesus had already started a small fire. There were fish cooking on the fire, and bread nearby.

Jesus turned to them with a warm smile. "Come and have breakfast," He said.

The disciples climbed out of the boat, their tiredness forgotten in the presence of Jesus. They sat down by the fire, the smell of the fish and bread filling the air. Jesus took the bread and gave it to them, and He did the same with the fish. It was a simple meal, but it was more than enough.

The disciples didn't ask Him who He was, because they knew. They knew it was Jesus, alive again, sitting with them, sharing a meal.

As they ate, Jesus spoke to Peter. "Simon, son of John, do you love Me more than these?" He asked.

Peter looked at Jesus, his heart full of love and gratitude. "Yes, Lord," he answered. "You know that I love You."

Jesus smiled and said, "Feed My lambs."

Then Jesus asked him a second time, "Simon, son of John, do you love Me?"

Peter was a little confused but answered, "Yes, Lord. You know that I love You."

Jesus replied, "Take care of My sheep."

A third time, Jesus asked, "Simon, son of John, do you love Me?"

Peter was hurt because Jesus had asked him three times, but he understood. Jesus wanted to make sure that Peter knew how deeply He cared for him and how much He trusted him. "Lord, You know all things," Peter said, his voice full of emotion. "You know that I love You."

Jesus smiled again, and with great compassion, He said, "Feed My sheep."

It was a beautiful moment. Peter had failed Jesus three times, just as Jesus had predicted. But now, Jesus was giving Peter three chances to declare his love for Him, to show that his heart was true. And with each "yes," Peter was restored. He was forgiven. He was given a new purpose.

Jesus had provided for them in a way they couldn't have imagined. He had shown them once again that He was always there, always ready to help, always ready to give second chances. And just as He had filled their nets with fish, He was now filling their hearts with His love and forgiveness.

As they finished their meal, Jesus looked at Peter and said, "Follow Me."

Peter, his heart full, knew exactly what Jesus meant. It was time to leave behind the old way of living, the old life he had known before. It was time to follow Jesus fully, no matter where it led.

And from that day forward, Peter would follow Jesus, spreading the good news of His love and forgiveness to others. He would be one of the leaders of the early church, helping to build the foundation of the faith that would spread throughout the world.

Chapter 18

Jesus Restores Peter

It was a quiet, peaceful morning by the Sea of Galilee. The smell of fresh fish and the crackling of a small fire filled the air as Jesus and His disciples sat together. The sun was rising, casting golden light over the water. It had been a long night, but now there was a sense of peace. They had shared a meal with Jesus, and their hearts were full.

But even in the stillness of that moment, Peter's heart was heavy. He remembered the night not long ago when he had denied Jesus three times. He remembered how he had promised, "I will never leave You," but then, when things got hard, he had been afraid. He had failed Jesus in the worst way. And yet, here Jesus was—alive, and sitting with him. Jesus had come back to forgive him, but still, Peter wondered if he could ever be truly forgiven.

Then, after they had finished their meal, Jesus turned to Peter.

"Simon, son of John," Jesus began, using Peter's full name, "do you love Me more than these?"

Peter's heart skipped a beat. Jesus was asking him something important. Peter looked into Jesus' eyes, those eyes full of love and compassion. Peter knew the answer. He had failed before, but now, his heart was changed. He had seen Jesus rise from the dead, and He had seen the forgiveness in Jesus' eyes.

"Yes, Lord," Peter replied, his voice steady but full of emotion. "You know that I love You."

Jesus smiled at Peter. He had asked a simple question, but there was so much more to it. He wasn't just asking about Peter's love for Him in that moment. He was asking Peter to show the world what love truly meant. So Jesus replied, "Feed My lambs."

Peter's heart lifted. "Feed My lambs," Jesus had said. This was more than just a command—it was a gift, a chance for Peter to serve. Jesus was restoring him, healing the hurt from his past, and giving him a new mission. Peter had denied Jesus three times, but now, Jesus was giving him three chances to declare his love for Him.

Then Jesus asked again, "Simon, son of John, do you love Me?"

This time, Peter's heart tightened. Why was Jesus asking him again? Didn't He already know that Peter loved Him? But still, Peter answered with all the honesty he had: "Yes, Lord, You know that I love You."

Jesus looked at Peter, His eyes filled with love and understanding. "Take care of My sheep," He said.

Peter felt his heart begin to heal. This was Jesus, the one who knew everything about him—the good and the bad. Jesus knew how much Peter had failed, but He didn't hold it against him. Jesus wasn't just forgiving him—He was restoring him, giving him a new purpose, a new way to serve. Jesus was showing Peter that love wasn't just something to feel; it was something to do.

But Jesus wasn't done. He asked Peter one more time.

"Simon, son of John, do you love Me?"

Peter was hurt this time. He knew why Jesus had asked him three times. Three times Peter had denied Jesus. But now, three times Jesus was giving him a chance to speak the truth.

Peter's voice trembled a little as he answered, "Lord, You know all things. You know that I love You."

Jesus smiled at Peter again, His heart full of love and compassion. "Feed My sheep," He said.

Peter's heart swelled. In these three questions, Jesus had not only forgiven him—He had restored him. Peter was no longer the man who had denied Jesus in the courtyard. He was now the man whom Jesus trusted, the man He had chosen to lead and care for His people. Peter had been given a mission, a purpose, and a second chance.

For Peter, this moment was more than just words. It was a transformation. Jesus had not only forgiven his failure, He had given him a new beginning. The pain of the past was still there, but it was no longer the most important thing. What mattered now was that Peter had been restored. Jesus had healed his heart, and now Peter could go and share that love with others.

Jesus knew that Peter would face hard times ahead. He knew that Peter would have to make difficult choices, and that he would experience challenges in his life. But in this moment, Jesus gave Peter the strength he needed to continue. Jesus gave him a calling to take care of others, to lead with love and humility, and to never forget the forgiveness and grace he had received.

And so, Peter was not just forgiven. He was redeemed. He was given a mission. And from that moment on, Peter's life would be forever changed. Jesus had not just healed him from the pain of his past; He had set him on a path of hope and purpose for the future.

As the sun continued to rise over the Sea of Galilee, Peter sat there, beside Jesus, knowing that he had been loved and forgiven in a way he could never fully explain. And with that love, he would go out and share the good news of Jesus' grace with the world.

Chapter 19
Jesus Gives the Great Commission

The disciples gathered together on a hill in Galilee, just as Jesus had told them. They were excited but also a little confused. They had seen Jesus die, and they had seen Him rise from the dead. But what did all of this mean for them? What were they supposed to do next? They waited, looking at each other with questions in their eyes.

Suddenly, Jesus appeared before them, His presence so powerful that it filled their hearts with joy. He had risen from the dead, and now He was standing before them, alive! His voice was calm, but His words were full of purpose.

"Go and make disciples of all nations," He said. The disciples could hardly believe what they were hearing. Jesus wanted them to go everywhere, all around the world, and share the good news about Him? But Jesus wasn't finished.

"Baptize them in the name of the Father, and of the Son, and of the Holy Spirit," He continued. "Teach them to obey everything I have commanded you."

The disciples' hearts raced as they realized what Jesus was asking. This was big! It wasn't just for the people they knew or the places they had been. Jesus wanted them to go to all nations—to people they had never met and places they had never gone. They were to spread the message of God's love everywhere.

But as overwhelming as this might have seemed, Jesus didn't leave them to do it alone. He promised them something incredible. "And surely I am with you always, to the very end of the age," He said, His voice filled with the certainty of His love.

The disciples stared at Him in awe. They had witnessed His death and resurrection, and now He was sending them out with a mission—a mission that would change the world. They were being called to share the message of Jesus' love with everyone they met, from the smallest village to the largest city. And they weren't going to be alone in this. Jesus Himself would be with them every step of the way.

As the disciples listened, they could feel their hearts burning with a new sense of purpose. They had walked with Jesus for three years. They had learned from Him. They had seen His miracles and felt His love. And now, He was telling them to share that love with everyone.

But how would they do it? How could they possibly go to all nations? They were just a small group of fishermen, tax collectors, and everyday people. Yet, Jesus wasn't asking them to do it by their own strength. He was giving them everything they needed: His power, His Holy Spirit, and His presence with them always. They were not just to go out in their own power, but in the power of God.

Jesus' words were not just for His disciples back then. They were for us today. The Great Commission is the same call Jesus gave to His followers then and still gives to us now. We, too, are called to share the good news of Jesus with the world. And we, too, are promised that Jesus will be with us always, even to the end of the age.

As the disciples stood there on that hill, listening to Jesus' final words to them, they knew their lives would never be the same. They couldn't keep the love of Jesus to themselves anymore. It had to be shared. They had seen the miracles, they had felt His love, and now they were called to tell the world. They were called to go everywhere and share the good news of Jesus.

And so, with hearts full of excitement and courage, the disciples took Jesus' words to heart. They began to go to all corners of the earth, sharing the message of Jesus. They told everyone they met that Jesus had died for them, that He had risen again, and that He loved them. And they baptized people in the name of the Father, the Son, and the Holy Spirit, just as Jesus had commanded.

The disciples weren't alone in this mission. The Holy Spirit was with them, guiding them, strengthening them, and empowering them to do the work that Jesus had given them. They were part of something bigger than themselves—a mission to share God's love with the whole world.

As they went, they faced many challenges. They were rejected, they were misunderstood, and sometimes they were even thrown into prison. But nothing could stop them. The message of Jesus was too powerful, and the love they had experienced was too amazing to keep to themselves. They knew that Jesus was with them, just as He had promised, and that gave them the courage to keep going.

And so, the disciples began a journey that would spread the good news of Jesus all over the world. From Jerusalem to Judea, to Samaria and beyond, they went. And every time they shared the gospel, the love of God grew stronger and stronger. People's lives were changed, hearts were healed, and the church grew.

But the mission wasn't just for the disciples; it's for us too. Jesus gave us the same Great Commission: to go and make disciples of all nations, to teach people about Jesus, and to baptize them in the name of the Father, the Son, and the Holy Spirit. We are all called to be part of this incredible mission.

As we go about our lives, we are called to share the good news of Jesus with others. Whether at school, at work, with our friends, or with our families, we are to tell others about Jesus and His love. And just like the disciples, we are promised that Jesus will be with us every step of the way.

So, whenever we feel unsure or afraid, we can remember Jesus' words: "Surely I am with you always, to the very end of the age." No matter where we go or what we face, Jesus is with us. He will give us the strength we need, and He will guide us as we share His love with the world.

The Great Commission is not just for a few people—it's for everyone who believes in Jesus. We are all part of God's plan to share His love with the world. And with Jesus by our side, we can be brave, we can be strong, and we can share the good news of Jesus with everyone we meet.

Chapter 20
The Ascension of Jesus

After Jesus had spent some time with His disciples after He rose from the dead, He knew the time had come for Him to return to His Father in heaven. So, He called His friends together one last time. They climbed a small hill in Galilee, looking out over the beautiful land where they had spent so much time with Him.

The disciples were eager to hear what Jesus had to say. They had learned so much from Him, and they had so many questions. Would He stay with them forever? What would happen next? What would the future hold?

Jesus smiled at them and said, "Soon you will receive the Holy Spirit. He will give you the strength and the courage to tell people everywhere about Me. You will be My witnesses, sharing My love with the world."

The disciples tried to understand, but there was so much to take in. Jesus had always been with them, guiding them, teaching them, and now He was saying they would carry His message to the world. It sounded like a big job, and they weren't sure if they were ready.

But Jesus assured them, "Don't worry. I will always be with you, even though you can't see Me. The Holy Spirit will help you, and I'll never leave you."

Then, something incredible happened. As they stood there listening, Jesus began to rise up, higher and higher, right before their eyes! The disciples gasped in amazement as Jesus floated up into the sky, moving further and further away from them. They couldn't believe what they were seeing! It was like something out of a dream.

"Where is He going?" one of the disciples asked.

But just as they were wondering, something even more surprising happened. Two men in shining clothes appeared beside them. The disciples stared at them in wonder.

"Why are you standing here looking up at the sky?" one of the men asked. "Jesus, who has been taken from you into heaven, will come back in the same way you saw Him go."

The disciples stared at each other. Did the men mean that Jesus was going to come back? They didn't know when, but the message was clear. Jesus was going to return, just like He had left, and they had a job to do while they waited for that day.

With hearts full of excitement and wonder, the disciples began to walk back toward Jerusalem. They had just witnessed something extraordinary—Jesus rising into the sky—and now they had a new mission to carry out. They had to go and tell everyone about Jesus and His love. And they had to do it with the confidence that Jesus would be with them through the Holy Spirit.

As they walked, the disciples didn't fully understand everything that had just happened, but one thing was certain—Jesus was still with them. He had promised to send the Holy Spirit, and the Holy Spirit would be their helper, guiding them as they went to share His good news.

And so, as the disciples returned to Jerusalem, they were filled with hope. They didn't know when Jesus would return, but they knew He would. And until that day, they had work to do. They were going to share the message of Jesus with the world, and they were going to do it with His help.

Even though they couldn't see Jesus with their eyes anymore, they knew He was still with them. He had given them everything they needed—His love, His teachings, and His Holy Spirit. They didn't have to worry, because Jesus had promised He would be with them always.

For us, just like the disciples, the promise of Jesus' return gives us hope. He is coming back one day to make everything right, and until that day, we are called to share His love with others. We don't have to do it alone—Jesus has sent the Holy Spirit to be with us, just as He promised.

So, while we wait for that glorious day when Jesus will return, we can live with joy, knowing He is always with us. And just like the disciples, we are called to tell the world about Jesus, the Savior who loves us and will return to bring us to live with Him forever.

Made in United States
Cleveland, OH
09 April 2025